Also by Roland Flint

And Morning
Say It

RESUMING GREEN

RESUMING GREEN

SELECTED POEMS, 1965 — 1982 BY

ROLAND FLINT

THE DIAL PRESS   NEW YORK

Published by
The Dial Press
1 Dag Hammarskjold Plaza
New York, New York 10017

"Glen Allen Delvo" was originally published in THE GEORGIA REVIEW, 1982.

"She Was Eight," "His Good Time," and "Earthworm" were originally published in *the minnesota review*.

"The Green for Pamela," "A Poem Called George, Sometimes," "Visit," and "Sabbatical" appeared originally in NUMEN: *New Southern Writing*, © 1980.

"Harrow Season Good-bye," "Amadeus Quartet," "Under Pressure Pigeon Stops Fighting It," and "Pigeon in the Night" first appeared in *Poet Lore*, a publication of the Helen Dwight Reid Educational Foundation, Summer 1981, pp. 93–102.

"Heads of the Children" first appeared in POETRY NORTHWEST, Autumn 1972, Vol. XIII, No. 3.

"Astrology," "Tulip Tree," and "Gift of Honey" first appeared in THE HONEY AND OTHER POEMS FOR ROSALIND (an Ampersand edition of Unicorn Publications: Huntington, West Virginia, 1976).

"Astrology" also appeared in SHAPING: *New Poems in Traditional Prosodies* (Dryad Press, 1978).

"To the Only Absolute Beauty Someone" first appeared in a souvenir postcard edition, published by the Friends of the Library, North Carolina Wesleyan College, 1981.

"Last Words," "Aubade," "He Didn't Even Know He Was A," "Pigeon Wonders Again," "God Bless Invention, Pigeon," "Nearing Their Official," and "It Seems That After Writing Twenty-Eight Days Without a Pause" were first published in *TriQuarterly*.

"Skin" first appeared in *Woodwind: A Journal for the Arts*.

"Prayer, Poor Sinners, Homely Girls" and "Turn" first appeared in *Dacotah Territory*.

"August From My Desk" first appeared in *The Atlantic Monthly*.

"Memento" first appeared in *Dryad Magazine*, 1975, in a special post-card issue.

"Rosalind October" first appeared in *Dakota Arts Quarterly*.

"Follow," "Name," "Shim," "Say It," "His Oyster," "Poem," and "Memento" first appeared in *Dryad*, #14 & 15.

The following poems appeared in *And Morning* (Dryad Press 1975): "Skin," "Follow," "Earth," "August From My Desk," "Turn," "Memento," "Prayer, Poor Sinners, Homely Girls," "She Was Eight," "His Good Time," "Wheel," and "And Morning In."

The following poems appeared in *Say It* (Dryad Press 1979): "Astrology"; "Shim"; "Gift of Honey"; "Spring Yellows for You"; "His Oyster"; "Fish Story"; "Shoe"; "Tulip Tree"; "Sabbatical"; "Paint"; "The Green for Pamela"; "A Poem Called George, Sometimes"; "Rosalind October"; "Visit"; "Rosalind's Poem for Beate and the Houseplants"; and "Say It."

Permission to reprint is gratefully acknowledged.

The author wishes to express his gratitude for the hospitality of the artists' colonies: Ossabaw, MacDowell, Yaddo, and the Virginia Center. He also wishes to acknowledge the support he received from the National Endowment for the Arts, in the form of a Discovery Grant in 1970 and a Fellowship in Creative Writing Grant in 1981.

Manufactured in the United States of America
First printing

Library of Congress Cataloging in Publication Data
Flint, Roland.
     Resuming green.
     I. Title.
PS3556.L56R4   1983   811'.54   82-12983
ISBN 0-385-27801-2
ISBN 0-385-27812-8 (pbk.)

To my parents, Orva and William

CONTENTS

RESUMING GREEN

SKIN

If the wood is good grain,
And the carpenter, the fit, the caulking,
The cask will be good
And if the grapes are good
The wood and the wine
Will improve each other,
In the dark long days of aging.

The separate tastes of earth
Will taste again and change again each other,
Until, like membrane, somehow
In and between the wood and wine
There will be no separation,
Wood from dark from wine.

When this goes on, anything can happen.
Go back, go back to mystery.
Now I am grateful to my small poem
For teaching me this again:
That my God is still the moment
Where the wood is no longer itself,
Where the wine is no longer, only, itself.

I

August
From My Desk

It is hot today, dry enough for cutting grain,
And I am drifting back to North Dakota
Where butterflies are all gone brown with wheat dust.

And where some boy,
Red-faced, sweating, chafed,
Too young to be dying this way,
Steers a laborious, self-propelled combine,
Dreaming of cities, and blizzards—
And airplanes.

With the white silk scarf of his sleeve
He shines and shines his goggles,
He checks his meters, checks his flaps,
Screams contact at his dreamless father,
He pulls back the stick,
Engines roaring,

And hurtles into the sun.

EARTHWORM

I think of a girl who hated to walk in the rain,
Loathing to step on them. I hope she got over that.
We liked to keep one on the sidewalk
And line it up with another
For an excruciating race,
Or to put it back in the grass
And watch its progress. Burrowing.

We said, when he's underground,
And worming, the earth goes right through him.

I still think of him that way, lank, blind,
Both ends open, refining whatever comes,
Dirt among rose roots, yeasty bodies.

He doesn't look for trouble. He just follows warmth,
At the earth's curve, coming up only for rain
And the feet of girls.

"If a son shall ask bread of any of you. . . ."

Father your voice was a fist
To slam my stomach shut
To start me from sleep like a rat,
You were the right and righteous anger,
Your voice made me believe
In God in the Devil.

When we meet now, forty and seventy,
You are apologetically quiet,
You put your arms around me
And I know you mean it.
We are both old men.

But I can only remember
Being held by you during beatings,
Which were not often but terrible,
And always worse, before them,
The fanatical white in your shouting.
I know, now, you didn't mean it.

But listen to me—
I'm doing the same thing
To my small son.
If my voice said what I mean
He could sleep all night in its branches,
But I hear your outrage in me,
Over nothing, a bare lie, or nothing,
And I see him cower for the storm cellar,
Just like me, his knuckles white with my yelling.
Father—I love you.
Jesus Christ, where does it end?

NAME

Did I half believe or all the sister
Who said I'd been left on the step,
Having been kidnapped somewhere by gypsies,
But eyes too dark even for gypsies,
Therefore left? or that
Any time they might be back
To claim me for the sign in my eyes
Of vagrancy? how dark I thought?

Junk the turning wheel and axletree,
The kettles junking hung from twine,
Junking and saying gypsy Roland,
Or foundling or poet in the name,
Oliver and pointing home
And Charlemagne the uncle.

Heavy and tall, she is her own cool beauty, but there are darker themes in those extraordinary breasts.

Like the long blonde hair and some secret, like hard crying, and like other great wonders of the world, except for these glimpses, I will never have them.

This morning, young, talented, and lazy, she brings another surprise, bearing, exactly, the smell of my grandmother.

I remind myself I have a head cold, but it's Grandma's smell all right, especially from the big, black dress-up purse, a combination of powder and perfume and some lozenge—not rose, though my grandmother's name was Rose.

I ask the girl to leave so I can let this petal and stem to its center.

Ever since an old dream, sometimes when I think of Grandma Rose, there is that boy, who comes running and calling in the tall cave, an underground depot or coal mine, calling and calling, as if the stone dark would somehow yield flint's rose.

He runs to sunken loading docks or great warehouses of gumbo—in the only light an angry man is candling eggs, one splats at my feet—the boy calls and calls and no one answers.

(Yes, I know about dark caves in dreams, purses, too, but I wish to tell you this.)

She was eighty-two when she died, after the endless floors and stories to change, cisterns and wells to empty and fill, and she was worn away, a perfect ancient child in her coffin, nothing left of the old roses, to flower, or purse.

When the poor come far to bury, they must make

the most of it. So there were all the clumsy solaces, of cousins and whiskey and food, crying and laughing hard.

After the group pictures, the uncles and widows passed out shares of the hospital and funeral bills, which settled Rose Flint's estate.

I was twenty-five, older than this opulent girl, who bears me beauty, invention, grief, scents from another world this morning: wonder for the boy I see from middle age and wonder for Grandmother Rose as a girl.

Pisces is my sign:
I don't have to believe it all
To see the fish is mine:
Two-way fish without a will,
Knowing by swimming on,
Turned tail, turning head,
Salmon red or white as pine,
Circling the islands of the dead,
Fish you are my sign.

After crossing the sea at Passover,
He gave more fish, more bread.
His sign is Ichthus, fish,
And he was bread for centuries,
The fish between our lips
And the blue air in good-bye.

In Cana the gift was so the pair could do
A thing that swims beyond them,
Bread for our first communion: wine,
To say the blue air like the ocean
Marries us,
To say the fish moves in the ocean,
Breathing air,
To say the farmer planting grain
Looks up to hear the fish wind,
Christ himself, leaven and green,
Like yeast off the ocean,
Fish meal and wine of marrow.

Father, today I forgave that sinner myself his pain
For the homely girls hoodwinked and left,
For heavy girls crying the good-bye boy
Did lay them down in small-time pastures,
For the wide-nosed farmers' daughters
Who swung like lonely cows in town
And there were milked, stripped, and left,
Again, to brood and ruminate.

Yes I forgive him Father your pain of his past
As may please God the girls
And thrive.

He's twenty-two and left everything to come here and paint and this morning he thinks he wants to paint the sunrise again, so he must get up at four-thirty to gather and ready his gear: canvas, portable easel, a paint box with many paints and brushes, because he can't anticipate exactly the colors and textures of sunrise, and he knows that, and that is part of what he likes about painting it.

He knows the best place in this frozen town for watching the winter sunrise: it is the top floor of a girls' dormitory on the campus of a formerly all-women's college.

He looks like a student himself, and he knows it, and knows he will have no trouble getting in, and anyhow he is carrying all that unrefusable zeal and equipment and has those bright sunhungering eyes, slightly crazed.

The guard mistakes him for an ordinary part of the bright, cold ordinary morning: "Jesus, these kids are sonthin'—I mean they *never* sleep, ehnn? and they're screwin' *all* the time—I had a kid come up 'ere at five in the mornin', says he ain't got a girl here, says he's a *painter*—are you ready for this?—says he's gonna paint the *sunrise—bull*shit."

But he is, and he is all set up in time and he is ready when the sun begins, bright-eyed and nuts in his clarity, everything ready, very happy about what he thinks he is, which happens this time to be exactly what he is, ten stories of beautifully sleeping girls he has ascended through to find himself right here, on this perfect scaffolding of drowsing arms and legs, the lovely heads turned this way, or turning, light and dark, shin-

ing and tousled, all sighs and shapes of hollows and
color, resting and waiting too, and he is ready for the
sunrise, all his brushes and colors ready.

When I lie under the tall trees
At this time of year,
No leaves yet but the buds ready to break,
When the separate winds make whole branches
Move drift return sway,
I see every possible thing is here,
From the first stir of creation
To the slow unwinding hieratic floods,
Branches the shapes of grief or expectation,
Infantile and ancient in the same knot.
Branches naked as roots.

And I dream the branches into roots—
Turn the worlds around,
Try to imagine in what underground sea,
In what floating skies of humus
The rooted branches drift, dreaming,
Into what clouds of anthracite they stare,
The sea weed branches waved into the nitrogen silent
    water.

It makes me believe again
In mirror versions of the universe—
Somewhere another poet writing this,
Lying on his back facing the lovely
Unchanging secret at the center,
Wondering the other world, dreaming
His dream of me.

II

Rosalind
October

On a fence post the rooster simply
Saying to the sun our father
Hello old cock I'm up again
And so are you

He lives in Washington, D.C., and he goes all the way to Georgia by car, passing through Virginia, North Carolina, South Carolina, then through part of Georgia on his way down to Savannah, then he goes by bus through Savannah to Vernon View, then he goes by boat across bays and inlets and sounds of the Atlantic to Ossabaw Island, then he goes by station wagon to the main house, then he goes by pickup truck with Mr. Jimmie Willard Perkins (nicknamed Middleton) to a tidal river to fish two hours for trout, with no luck, then he goes by foot, with Middleton, one mile downriver through the woods to an oyster bed Middleton knows about, and there he finds an oyster—or a hard, gray-brown shell, covered with little stones and carbuncles that looks like it could be an oyster. He knows there is something in it he wants. He takes a razor-sharp knife that has come from Sweden for this (via Sears in D.C., trips to Maine, Vermont) and he tries to open this thing which has the brave, angry face of a petrified knish. It will not open. He takes a stone and taps easy, then hard, on the base of the handle, trying to drive it into the oyster—it doesn't work, the oyster slips away, sideways, he tries again and fails again, and then he blows up, and puts it on a big flat rock and pounds it with a stone, just trying to smash it, and that doesn't work, and he picks the sonofabitch up and throws it down as hard as he can and he thinks well now would be a goddamned good time for a miracle, for it to roll over and just open slowly and teach him something about the futility of violence, the shame of pride, the pride of anger, the surprise of faith where not to knock by Christ is open wide. Instead it stays tighter than a bull's ass in

fly-time, teaching him the horseshit of inwit, the agen-
bite and fuck you of fantasy, and the true kryptonite
hardness of an oyster you can't have even if you're Clark
Kent and have driven six hundred miles to get it. Mid-
dleton spits some Honey-cut and says, "ats fuckin oyrs-
ters."

At the outdoor party after someone else's wedding,
A girl came up to me, her champagne
Catching light like a handful of sun,
And she made a toast that permitted us
At the end of it, arms linked, to kiss,
And she brought me the memory of being loved—
A balance—failure behind,
Brought me herself, beside me all day,
The vellums and bread of her body,
The directness and blue of her eyes like flax.

The party and my urgency took us both away,
And now she has to get her balance
Between familiar and unfamiliar air—which I
        understand—
Between what we felt that day
(The exact name was love)
And the rock slides of
My age, my family, my self.
She has to look right at me
To say she has some plans of her own.

Besides, she says,
You were tipped toward need just then,
Starving all those ways, that any arms would do,
For a while, and for a while I think she's right,
But I'm not sure: it was not a dream, after all.

Anyway, she regrets as I do (a little differently)
The general failure of symmetry,
Not just the jagged collisions,
No means or no needs no blossom or no bee,

But that the world itself is bent,
Simple wholeness gone.

And she's wrong in thinking even she is flawed,
One leg a mother's whisper shorter than the other.
She needs me, too, my eyes to see
If there's a difference it's a bonus,
A lover's secret longer than the other.
She needs to see my mix of her,
High on a balance beam or poem
In the rich champagne of her skin,
Adjusting on one toe all the failures
Of exigency and symmetry,
A mix of durum wheat and air,
Of opulence and hurt.

I tried:
I told her only the true freaks are truly regular—
Like politicians, one side to the camera,
The other sinking doors to empire . . .
Or Hollywood, the plastic
Balance of whose breasts
Buoys and fills the dreams of millions—
Not mine, bread in mine or grass.

And so,
Though the next day was far down,
For gratitude I tell this generous girl,
Strange, maybe quick-tempered,
To love especially the gift
By which she knows the human shape,
The luck of imperfection—
A tremor in God's thumbs—
To be grateful as I am, deeply,
That the imprint took enough
To leave inside the news of general hurt.

It brought her to my side to say,
By being there, I see you and I know,
To say you're wrong only in thinking
Something's wrong with you,
To say if you fall I'll catch you,
To say, simply by being there,
Today I'm here to give you balance,
To shim and bind you—
I can do it freely and I want to do it:
Today I am the other half of you,
So you'll remember love,
And when you carry me I carry you.

Edge of April

It is five A.M. at March's end,
And still dark out,
With all the shades down.
But a spring bird has just made
A morning sound.
It grips the silence around my window
With a bright yellow hand,
The color of those roses I sent you
From Amarillo, and the bikinis
For your birthday, a bright yellow hand
Upon the winter of nights
Around me for months.
Thin yellow theft, prolepsis
Of the sun's descent
Sing.

May Letter

The beautiful small breasted woman
Comes in from the rain
Wearing those bright—bright!—and shiny
Yellow boots
And I think how I love yellow in flower or slickers
And how I love small breasted women
What a generosity it makes in them, of sex
And wearing yellow in the rain,
And I think, my small breasted love,
Of you, the clean and fragrant yellows
You wear to bed, daisy, corn, and the delicate

Yellow down inside of trillium,
How the ribbon bright and yellow
Of women with small breasts
In their rich inversion of what is generous
In the things of the world
Means they will not fade or fall
Away from love.

She brings me honey from New Zealand—
That's her home—
But she has to emigrate to get it,
New Zealand to here to London:
She buys it at Harrods in London.
She knows I love the thick,
Butter-colored honey
Of the country of her childhood and past,
Stronger than sweet, and denser,
What the Greeks must have had, *meli.*
She brings me two jars this time,
Enough to be a preservative—
Didn't the ancients use honey to sweeten death's
     bones,
To line and fill the memory of love?
And did it work?
But what will I do
With these two jars of her gift to me?
Isn't it a little more than I need?
Especially if a little more than a little
Is much too much.
Well I say maybe not,
If one has never had enough before,
And been given now a plenitude of honey,
On which the labels say just
Honey   New Zealand.

She and my daughter at the wheel
Making an ordinary cup (for me)
Gather with the clay into
The whirlpooling in and down
To the center of clay
And against that drying earth—
My friend and daughter pulled away—
I stare and darken.

She calls this part throwing it—
Which sounds easy—
And which means
From a handful of clay
To make a standing space,
The eloquent steady gesture of hands
Making a shape to drink,
And it looks easy.

That's a clue because,
Though you might not do as well
The first time as my eight-year-old,
It *is* easy, once you know how.
So metaphors, journeymen to everything,
In the clay's wet shape of palms.
But I try and do tell myself
That making a shape against death
Is at least as harmless as making a poem
And as much less poor
As I am able to drink from it.

Put on the high tough glazes,
Fire until it answers,

In blue and surface bite,
The sound—ceramic—
And it will cool
In infinite regress
Into some night
Of a cloud's slow shoulder roll
Against the invisibly wet and wheeling moon.

ROSALIND'S POEM
FOR BEATE AND THE HOUSEPLANTS

When people say listen to this, this would make a
perfect Flint poem, I do listen—for friendliness and be-
cause you can never tell.

But when Rosalind says something is worth a poem,
I get my pencil out. As if it's a secret between us like all
the poems secretly from her.

We left the house and plants with our German
friend, Beate. And when we returned, the television was
broken but the plants had grown a foot—in four weeks,
house trees, dieffenbachia, an African violet, the split-
leaf philodendron, many more.

In one abandoned planter in a corner of the porch
an ordinary weed was eighteen inches high.

She said, I just watered them regularly—but *we*
water them regularly. Surely she sang them German lul-
labies, or played them Handel's "Water Music," or put
them all around her bed at night and hummed some
secret incantation from her name.

I made many poor jokes to the woman in my first
life about her failure with indoor plants—they all quickly
withered or went on stunted and pale green.

Six months after *I'd* left, her downstairs looked like
a greenhouse. When I saw it that first time, all my stale
jokes just like my thumb went dog-turd brown in my
pocket.

But in my new life, even in my presence, there are
many plants, all growing and all green. An avocado seed
is a tree, four feet high, still growing. Everywhere I look
is green.

That's how the poems have grown around Rosa-
lind, like wild roses in a wood, where birds paint by,

composing the linden trees. Like the houseplants
around Beate.

So when Rosalind says there's a poem in Beate's weed in the abandoned planter, I believe her. And I believe I am that weed.

And I believe Beate when she says the TV just fell off its table one night while she was sleeping.

At last I have entered welcome
And touched the metaphor of welcome
To find myself healthy and strong as I thought.
The yearning doesn't stop,
But now I know there is enough
And I am worthy.

Soon I'll be forty years old
And I am broken, permanently,
In some ways I did not devise
And may not speak of.

But now there is a hurt ended,
Because someone, without righteousness,
Has welcomed me,
And it only has to happen once.

I think there should be something here
That has a harpsichord
Or censer
Or testament of holy loves.
Maybe that will come with time:
Now I feel simple gratitude
For being taken in and in and in.

Don't think I mean it less because I said metaphor.
Can't you tell how I love that shape,
That song in the language, metaphor?
Grain in a thumbprint for longing,
Memory in cirrus or barley,
Fright in driftwood—metaphor—

That has always let me in
As she has let me in.

Dear focus of silence
Beyond the last space in which to cut
The human shapes of welcome,
Mystery past but inviting metaphor,
Thank you most tonight for this song,
But also for that yearning in Adam's head
That tore a rag from the floor of his mouth
To be a tongue for me
To wrap around this song,
Passage, lintel, carriage light,
For participation, and ignorance,
And at last for perfect worthiness.

White my book, I'm back: in the yellow and cinnamon streets of mid-October the broken golds come down to say no wanwood lies: in autumn we begin again for the last time, and the trees are pulling music from the high wind and from the brightest light all year: Ravel and Mozart from the great masts of the flying trees.

So I tell the visiting friend, this must be a gift, which I am avid for, to walk from a dark transept to the middle again, to climb the steps at the center of the cruciform, in the steep cathedral of longing: *introibo.*

And the windy streets fly shining with the buckles of October, blues of the change I'm growing through, tough dull greens that have bitten down to stay, and red—and reds are falling down around me so I can hear and smell them red.

And now the old flower vendor calls out to me: these are nice, she says—yes, I'll take them; and these are nice—I'll take them too; and so are these—fine, I'll take them.

Chrysanthemums, corn marigolds and ox-eye daisies.

They say a name I want to hear when hers is crossed with mine, and if we make a house inside this old October's blowing, it's her name too and she will hear it too.

III

March Winter,
February Spring

After she had witnessed and somehow survived her twin brother's death, my daughter Pamela and I would lie across the bed, staring out the window at dusk, and see what human faces and animal shapes we could see or make in the waving green tops of the darkening trees.

When the streetlights came on, it was different, and beautiful still: the leaves, resuming green, were on our side of the lamp, the light lighting the tree and shining through to us, like daytime—cleaner, though, and greener.

But it was best just before the lights came on: we would be there and talk and wait for a little dark and a little wind to make the trees move and sough and whisper as they rearranged the human faces and animal shapes of night—an elephant nodding, a dog wagging or leaping, Mr. Bishop's face in Mr. Bishop's tree.

It's been three years and I don't remember now if I knew those nights I was leaving, I don't think so. But we had already left the happy shouting, the dancing, wrestling and marching games before bed.

And we were looking for a quiet way to translate night into the green human faces and animal shapes we knew to move in the sun all day and to wait all night for our return, resuming green.

Having lent my apartment to visiting friends,
I was sleeping in a strange basement
And I was wakened by a crumb in my ear—
I tried to shake it out, tossing my head.
No luck. It was not a crumb.
Though I didn't know it yet, it was a bug.
Not small. So burrowed in
My friend couldn't see it
When I finally called her to look.
Sweating-cold, crazed, thinking of death,
Feeling it move, deeper, gurgling, in and in—
I poured water in to drown it,
And pried it out with a cuticle knife.
Pure dread—I was awake for hours.

Late the next day I was telling
How fine the previous day had been,
How wrong to end like that.
And then slowly, and then suddenly,
I realized what the thing in my ear had said.
It said, *listen,* this will make you hear
What kind of day it was:
Slow, and warm, and fine,
A two-mile run in the rain,
A new book on the great Jefferson begun,
People pleased with your own book, proofs!
Children laughing, calling.

And most good, and, at the start of your fifth decade,
Most strange,
A beautiful woman loves you so

The dank corners lighten,
Listen—

How she came to you at noon with love,
How you went to her at night for love,
And found the light was in you, singing.

I couldn't hear it until now,
The brown, ugly, implacable bug saying
Pay attention: this is back of any perfect day,
Madness, the child's death, and will not stop,
And saying, by the difference,
Will you hear, now, which side of days you have.

Then thank a mystery that speaks your name,
Thank every trick in your ear, and listen.

Patsy Murphy had red knuckles
From marble games
And went coatless in winter,
Early and late.

When she died
We went to see her
In her inevitable pink coffin,
And tried to think of missing her.
I envied the Catholics, busy with their hands.
She was eight.

Now is a time
Of crippled sounds through the soft air,
Of doves making summer grief,
Of leghorns flapping anger at the sky.

Here on the prairie, our dream of ocean,
We can see the sun all day,
And watch the moon stand up,
Flowers open, flowers close.

No flower, nothing delicate . . .
Implicit in her features, all too large,
Was beauty,
Her grudging fudging marble skill
Said woman, strong.

In reluctant prairie trees outside
The grass makes small obeisance to a stream
That is reaching for the sea,
Leaves cartwheeling on its back,

While minutely speckled minnows sweep
Silently, and swift as gulls.

My face is growing smaller.

Patricia my classmate has been dead
For twenty years.

What am I sleeping to on these days, a sabbatical in the second year of my fifth decade—*fifth* is what I mean to write, but I almost write *last*.

I've never slept so much, so well, so long and dreamless as now, the last two weeks.

I've come north from a February spring in Georgia to this March winter and the reverse has spun me back to something, a phase of infancy or some new prenatal term, some getting ready again.

I roll to the crook of my sleep and stay, in the dark comfort of some innocent change I'm turning to.

This could be the last great sleep of youth, a menopausal sleep, the last innocence and separation to the final wakefulness of age, the drifting snow to the rickety laths of a fence I'll never see—that is, if it is a sleep at all and not the permanent insomnia in the corner of an eye—whose eye?

I think of Grandma Dvorak reading from her Czech bible all night long, rocking back and forth, moaning, davening, telling the air around her, "I'm ready for Jesus, unhhh, I'm ready for Jesus."

What tries to sneak in here and say this is my last ten years? I am not ready for Jesus.

No: I sleep because I can. It has taken me almost three months to feel no deadlines, no deadlines, the lumped failure in my neck when the daily bread is chewing.

The last dream I remember, before the Sabbath rest came down, I was running scared to give a talk I'd never heard of, something heavy pulling the left side.

But after three months I have found my drowsy

holiday, my first three months without a job since the
fifth or sixth grade.

After how many years on the stones of that scent—
a dampness on copper, must of clarinets, the spit-metal
smells of fear—after all these years I have found the boy
to sleep. So soundly and full and soft I don't get up at
all until morning and then I have to hurry and almost
do that adolescent handstand to make my water.

In the five hour sleeps of my other life, I'm up al-
most every hour to worry and dribble.

Yesterday I had a long walk, and a nap, and I slept
nine hours last night.

This morning I had oatmeal for breakfast, the snow
is so deep.

The drunk man in the new hat is red,
Or darker, the permanent corner
Slurring among our blondes.
And Aborigines drink badly in Australia,
In New Zealand the Maoris, where shadows of them,
Darker, the Morioris, who ate insects and honey,
Were so black that nobody drinks like that.

But every light skin needs a drunken Indian
To lug around the dark it fears
To give strong drink to:
So he can drink without a worry—
He won't get drunk . . . some Indian will.

And sure enough, some Indian will,
In a new hat, wild and drunk
In Sioux Falls on Saturday night,
With a knife in his hand.

Because why not?
Indian is as Indian does
And does it right up here in front
To be himself for him—and for me too.

(Will you have just a taste, Mr. Hyde?—
I wouldn't if I were you)

Listen: the Little Big Horn was a whiskey jug,
Those crazy bastards were drunk,
Killing themselves, killing us—and
They didn't sober up till Wounded Knee.

In Minnesota tonight the beautiful Scandinavians
Are drinking a river of beer and aquavit:
A red man in an old hat
Sits naked in his dugout,
The dark sun
Dark along his spine,
He's going nowhere away,
But always inland
To sow and blossom white.

Where is his mind, the old Greek farmer at the bar?
His son and young wife stand, while he sits,
Drinking from the bottle with closed lips.
They know he's crazy, and mugging, they tell the
        bartender,
Who is looking up from the glass the old man shoved
        away.
He doesn't speak, but he buys the round.

They flank him and watch the coin purse
        unpuckering,
When he squeezes it, like something obscene.
Crazy, but he holds the money and knows amounts.
Therefore do his kin stand ready, contemptuous
But patient, as he presses his index finger to his ear,
His cheek, his nose, or holds it up and looks
At it, smiling, sucking his beer and humming.

He dreams the footpaths in Crete,
The contrition of a young wife, her head held so,
The caves of the sea at night, his catechism,
A son born in a cave of sod, the endless earth of North
        Dakota
The clapboard rising at last . . . in the sea,
The blade breaking into new ground, his ground,
Into . . . her head held so, his last wife.
And she stands patient now
As he presses his ear, cheek, nose,
Or hums to his finger a vague falsetto,
Deeds, documents and unforgivables
With the coin purse in his breast.

They've known his mind is gone since they found him,
In the cold night, wearing only his long johns,
A pitchfork in his hands, cleaning the barn in the dark.
They watched him and laughed with relief,
The old man grinning back and nodding emptily.
But he surprised them by keeping a hard clear place
For the money, paying bills in cash, not speaking.

This is his good time, out of hurt but in charge,
Before someone whispers power of attorney.
And someone will.

But what did their faces do
The first time they tried to take him
And he blazed up clutching that coin purse—
Odysseus, crazy, dressed like a bum
And stringing the bow.

Now here is this man mending his nets
After a long day, his fingers
Nicked, here and there, by ropes and hooks
Pain like tomorrow in the small of his back,
His feet blue with his name, stinking of baits,
His mind on a pint and supper—nothing else—
A man who describes the settled shape
Of his life every time his hands
Make and snug a perfect knot.

I want to understand, if only for the story,
How a man like this,
A man like my father in harvest,
Like Bunk MacVane in the stench of lobstering,
Or a teamster, a steelworker,
How an ordinary working stiff,
Even a high-tempered one,
Could just be called away.

It's only in one account
He first brings in a netful—
In all the others, he just calls,
They return the look or stare and then
They "straightaway" leave their nets to follow.
That's all there is. *You* have to figure
What was in that call, that look.

(And I wouldn't try it on a tired working man
Unless I *was* God's son—
He'd kick your ass right off the pier.)

If they had been vagrants,
Poets, or minstrels, I'd understand that,
Men who would follow a different dog.
But how does a man whose movement,
Day after day after day,
Absolutely trusts the shape it fills
Put everything down and walk away?

I'd pass up all the fancy stunting
With Lazarus and the lepers
To see that one.

I'm at a kind of country inn and get to know the shoes and walking sounds of complete strangers. I wouldn't notice this but for an old woman here, all of whose shoes squeak.

What makes an old woman's shoes squeak?

Where she lives and walks is there heavy dew that does something to leather? Maybe she lives in a city and walking on concrete flattens them but tunes their resistance?

Old or new, they sound like leather feet, even the slippers, leather on leather. So squeak is the wrong word, too timid, high, mousy, too squeaky.

The exact sound, especially from the black Capezios, is the sound from a western saddle when you put all your weight in the first stirrup.

It's as if her big German feet fear a Chinese indignity, and so always get into shoes a size too big. Her feet slide and catch in them as if hostile to walking on other skins, or as if angry with all dependencies that strap us to our bindings.

The poor leather in those old shoes. How long has it been unpliant, walked into stiffness by stiffness, and the poor old unreconciled leather of those poor old feet—still raging, maybe, at a lover's obsession with a long second toe.

She has a look of kindness in her face, but even there is something raw and unsettled—at eighty—some sexual hunger or anger or hurt, never settled. There is a hard grace too in her size and erectness. She has hands like a stevedore and wears a man's hat. So she enters, her shoes squawking, as if, under her dignity, they say for her:

Of course my shoes make noises—who are you? Do you know how many miles I've walked? what things I've had to walk on? what I've stepped in? walked in upon? accidentally or deliberately kicked? Forgive or not the cowhide noises of an old woman's feet. I have walked so far and I want to walk so far.

Angels can walk in gravel and make no noise: but here is a woman who has settled with specific gravity into leather of her mortal flesh, a life that has groaned through its subcutaneous muffling and into the bone.

If death himself slipped in one day when she was dozing, and tried to take back the shoes, she jumped up, scared and angry, and yelling to keep them, and she goes on in that terrible fury to live, which survives and will survive her dead, outrageous, noisy feet.

I'm sitting at a glass-topped table under a tulip tree whose blooming my new friend Nellie and I have made our predictions on.

It is February, this is Georgia, and yesterday for the first time we had eighty degrees.

I am out here in the bright, warm day, liking it, and without warning I miss my son, not only in the usual ways but with a kind of wonder that it persists so hard and long and that it is so physical, that I want to hold and feel him in my hands and arms, and that my grief at its worst still is something in my chest like the dreams that go on hurting but you want them as all you have left.

And part of a sheath, the covering of a tulip bud, falls onto the table by my right hand.

It is a color between ripe pear and chamois, very delicate, covered with the fur of a small creature, more than on a peach.

Inside it is smooth and feels like the inside of a kitten's ear, exactly.

There is no special providence in this, I think, but I am grateful anyway that the sheath is simple and useful and beautiful, that I know it, and that I like very much its falling here on my table and that it means the tulip tree will bloom when Nellie said it would, which is fine with me, because it is even sooner than I guessed.

Before he died, my son made up this poem:

There once was a boy
Who went to the market
And bought some hot chocolate
And put it in his red pocket.

I said, it's fine, Ethan, especially that red pocket—
what do you call it? He said, what do you mean? Most
poems have names, I said. And he said, ah . . . George.

And when he heard me repeating the story of his
poem and of its naming, he said, sometimes I call it
Jack.

That wasn't his best poem. Like me he didn't in-
tend his best poem: we were walking beside the tidal
basin just past dawn, the cherry trees in bloom, the sun
bright and the blossoms reflected in the still water. He
pointed down and said,

Look, water in the trees

I thought I would steal the title, my lost boy, to be
with you in your poem, but it's made me see I'm going
to have to write that poem I do not want to write, named
Ethan.

IV

The Pigeon:
Staying On Behind

Pigeon: until the day in New York City
When he'd left the rented nest & her
He's often called a nest & was walking,
Bad hungover from the pre-wedding bash
To his favorite Wolf's (52nd & 7th)
For bagel, egg & aspirin,
And his path was blocked by
Pigeons & then just one,
Fat, rumpled, grouchy, clumsy,
And he & the pigeon did
A little dance before finding
The paths around, & he thought
Oh God, I danced like that last night
At the fancy dinner, dressed just
Like a pigeon in the rented tux,
Colliding with the bride's mother,
Saying some dumb pigeon-yiddish, & pigeon
Dancing, drunk & bumbling,
Stumbling by: pigeon, plain
As pigeon.

Feels a little black hole in his chest
And knows it to be his heart,
Dense with the gravid night,
A black invisible diamond weighing in
With the accumulation of its losses,
The cruel impacted build-up, the loss
Especially this morning, drawing all the others into it,
Of his own right hand, his heart itself,
For a while, his son gone forever.
He can't quite hang on to pigeon when
The night bores in like this.

Pigeon skipped a day & woke
With childhood feelings of, he'll call it,
Giantism, as he lay too full
And half-boozed still
All the massy old enormous pressure
On his wings which felt
To pigeon in the dark
Pterodactyl at least, the
Claws he rubbed together or
Scrubbed the perch with even bigger
And pigeon trying not to ignore it,
Sleep it away as he used when he was little,
Scared, but trying to hold it now,
Stay to see what it is:
Memory of birthing in the
Clotted channel—*squeezed*. . . ?
Source of pigeon claustrophobia for sure.
It's a feeling pigeon hadn't had for
Fifteen, twenty years & which
Used to be very bad: moon or beach on pigeon
Little. *But* is probably also related
To his impulse, always, to turn off
The elevator lights, grasp the waist-high
Railing in his claws & perch a little
As down the sliding dark,
Pigeon flies the sea.

TO THE ONLY ABSOLUTE
BEAUTY SOMEONE

Is sending roses anonymously
And pigeon wishes it were he—
Oh maybe you know (by your light)
A beauty *you* think perfect, but
The pigeon doubts, trusting his eye,
There is another one like this: no vellums
Or oven-bread or delicacy from flax
Can take a flesh this tone,
No metaphor to gather hair up in the back so
Soft, thick, auburn-red &
Radiantly sexed withal,
Spain in the blood someplace, & a nun, & Capri.
And, hilarious to p, she doesn't *know:*
He sees she thinks she's bone & ghost
A certain flash to men. Well listen:
General Motors & NASA
And all the nuclear power plants, the temples,
The cloud-capped towers
And the great globe itself could buzz
A year at least if we could turn
Libido that burns for her
(Or has) to lignite or uranium or
The blood-black oil of ancient birds,
From whom, irrelevantly,
Descends at last admiring p,
Who thinks, by God, *some*body knows
The perfect flower for her, blood red: *a rose.*

If an ordinary pigeon can
Make a nest to last forever.
OK, not forever really or even
Within three or four
Methuselahs of Hector but
Till Thursday, say, or
The end of the summer, century or so.
Whether it's possible on the tops of low
Buildings or in open eaves, old-house cupolas,
To make, with sticks & strings & grass,
Saliva for stickum &
Essential if deliberate dirt
Something for comfort, lying
Down in, hatching, eventually,
All the rest.
And how it all might look from there:
Green & good, thinks pigeon.
No wonder
At all, it's time to go down again
And do the pigeon things.

Coming back some from his loved friend's death,
Greeting the day again, scratching around, &
News comes another old friend is dead,
Bringing the year's total to four from cancer alone
And so the pigeon flies northwest to be there,
His heart aburst with emptiness to witness
His poor old friend all dead & coffined,
To comfort as well as he can the widow & child
To carry his friend to the terrible hole
To eat & drink too much (with grief to blame it on)
To visit his aging parents
To take them out to dinner
To cut his broken-wristed father's steak
To stay two days & nights & mow his mother's lawn
To speak carefully with them of the bereaved
To toss all night in the creaking bed
In which he was conceived.

Says, because
When his lady's broken thigh
Was, though mending, muscle-knotted
Like a fist (her size)
And, as she lay beside him,
After dinner having tea,
Kneading it gingerly with her left hand,
Then invention came a little,
Giving him the metal teapot,
Hot but not too hot (through the sheet)
To iron the knot out, steady & hard,
Agitato ma non troppo,
For half an hour.
Pigeon says God bless it because
Her leg felt better all night
To let her sleep, for a change,
And also bless invention for
The ways she rubbed him back:
Now *there's* a rub, by God.
God bless it too—& does.

First Anniversary pigeon remembers
What was, maybe, their first one,
Unofficial, when they were a year
In flesh, or so, but new in love,
Or, anyway, the pigeon's lady knew it
(So she says) & pigeon was starting to suspect,
At least, that this was it.
Nearing this date six years later
Pigeon thinks she is the only girl in the
Truest sense he's ever had:
For nests & bests & bads & all,
The firsts for each enough
Despite the other lives & (partial) many loves,
And saying it reminds him of that day
Six years or so ago when she
Was telling him of her home, New Zealand:
South Island, North Island, Maoris,
Morioris, geysers, glaciers, green mountains & steam,
And how, small as it is, & known,
"There are still parts," she said,
Blushing a little & looking up to him like a question,
That he should understand it to be literal, "there are
Still parts of the country no one has explored."
In New Zealand secrets of the heart they go,
Lady & pigeon, & find it so.

And gives thanks to the great darkness
Before which he is stupid & reverent,
The sung silence to every question
He no longer asks, wide-eyed, in those cupolas
On the night he roosts in, content,
But frightened still: & prays his heart out
It won't test him in that final way
He has addressed the dark about
In gravest secret, darkest doubt,
Because with all his heart he fears
That test (another time) could break
In half or more his faith & will
To love his life &, worse, he fears
It *wouldn't:* if he survived that death
He'd somehow never love the simple life
Or stupid faith in dark again,
All suspect, all fugitive, survivors
On offal. But still he knows he errs
In this—scared & furious at the *chance,*
Just as, at last, he knows the dark, how it's
Beyond his power or wish to argue—& submits.

PIGEON SEES HOW THIS
            SCRATCHING OF HIS

Will be more & more the center:
Family & friends he loves are dying
Of hearts or falling, pills or cancer,
And as long as pigeon is staying
On behind (& long he means & wants
To do) he must always chance
And court the dumbest failures of saying
(Almost) exactly what he means. He's not praying
For miracles or lost in some delusion
He'll get out alive, or even (for long) survive
This ugly place he loves in rapt confusion.

V

Harrow Season

We'll never know what happened between him and that .22, except the final thing: dead in his room, somehow by his own eleven-year-old hand: dropping it? scuttling to hide it before his angry father found him with it, loaded? fumbling to get the cartridge out? scared and clumsy, hearing the old man coming down the hall yelling his nickname, *Mike*?—or, full of boyish rage and, getting it ready, accidentally shooting it?

Or in some quick, long, terrible vision spinning from the past and from the long and terrible future, did he stop in that room away from his age and place and expectation and turn it all around to close and open everything at once?

Daredevil Mike, he was the only one, when we went to the great barn to catch pigeons, who dared to cross the center of the hay mow, hanging by his hands and knees to make the fat birds fly our way.

A year or so later his grown-up brother, Shorty, maybe a little tight, caught me at a basketball game, red-faced, pleading, and held my arm, and told me, "Wasn't Mike a happy kid? He was always such a happy kid, wasn't he?"

I guess I said yes, because I guess I thought he was, but what I wanted to say was, *Let go.*

It's been more than thirty years and I wish I had been more help, Shorty, because now I know in spades. Louie and Lefty and Ivan and Jim and you are gone as well. And Mike is still vivid and dead to me as he was to you the night you caught me.

Sometimes I don't know how we do it.

The sun's insinuations
Breathe frozen fissures soft,
Greening trees, breaking blossoms,
Sliding winter down.

No spring has ever
Tempered its harrow teeth as innocent
Or sunk as deep as this.

At noon the doves do not begin to mourn,
Lost in leaves, distance, song,
The small birds too don't keen
But charm the needle spring.

When the dogwood blossoms start to glow
A squirrel chatters dusk
Where he is joined to dig
And change this hour
If he could.

1

When the tornado hit, this man was home, because he is retired, and he and his wife are watching TV in the living room. He goes to check the bedroom windows and the tornado sent a tree down on the house, on the bedroom, and on the man at the window.

His wife ran in to him and he called out to her: *Get back honey—I'm crushed.*

And I reach like this in my dark to a man with the everyday honey and warning in his last good-bye.

2

When the fifteen-year-old runaway was found in the alley far down from the window she'd been thrown from, the father in Ohio came to identify and take her home.

And when he'd seen her, he said: *She look like she been picked up and dropped—broke like glass.*

And it made me think of the brother in a play who wants his sister dead and then he sees his sister dead and says: *Mine eyes dazzle, she died young.*

3

When Bob the aging poet's wife was dying at home, this last thing happened: they were home because she wished it, they still loved each other, were a comfort in being there, but also in jokes and stories, reminiscences and badinage, as always.

Her name was Chris and one day near the end when she called him from the other room and motioned him to the bed, they had this talk:

There's something I want to tell you, Bob.

What is it, dear?

It's not easy to say but I feel I should tell you now.

Well whatever it is, you know *you can tell me, Chris,* Please.

He leaned over then and she said to him: *You can't sing worth a damn, Bob.*

And at the memorial service when the sorrow and sad speeches grew too much for him, Bob says, he got up and told that story, and they all laughed and went home.

Fishing Ossabaw the first time I was lucky, catching a beautiful trout on my first cast, a fish with big blue stipples, backed with a color so purple it was nearly violet, and with that luminous fish-silver shading into plain white along its belly.

It was only three or four pounds but it was the biggest fish I'd ever caught, and I caught it, as I said, fishing Ossabaw, which has a reputation for mystery, tree-spirits, the plat-eye, hags in their own time hollering the night out, and, by the way, for bass that often go better than ten pounds, trout better than five.

But I bragged, telling someone, "I'm lucky at fishing and poker," implying love, sex, poetry. I really may have believed that all that blue and silver I had caught was created, hooked and landed by some magic of my own. And though I've gone nine or ten times now and though I have stayed from two to four hours each time, I haven't caught a damned thing since, and I think I'm beginning to get it.

Today I fished with a kind woman named Agnes, who gave me a lure the color of her own, showed me where to cast, even moved down the bank so I could cast out there where the fish were and where, finally, Agnes took seventeen trout, small, but trout, and beautiful.

And I mean it—when she was pulling them in with nearly every cast, sometimes our lines would cross out there, in the middle of a school, ravenous! And nothing for me . . . not even a bite.

So I think that I'm being told something—about the terms of bounty, say, or pride in a magic place, or maybe that for a while the question to fish is a place inside my head: it has tidal creeks and rivers too, where the marsh grass and the shade of fallen trees speak trout, sound bass and bait humility, where the living oaks, with captive spirits, a face like mine in the whorl and bark, lean into shadows filled with fish that may or may not bite.

Assume nothing now, except that if the line pulls back and the rod bends and jumps, the reason for it, that luck at the end of the line, is as hidden from me as the hook, as dark as the mystery in a mouth to take *that* ordinary lure and not to take this one.

There's an ending to this story, and it's true: on my way home I met another woman who cheered me up, saying maybe I'm meant to be lucky in poems, not fish—the same message on my slack line and bare hook.

I settle for that, fished to the end of a long page, my first in many days, and I feel better now.

When you make a coat of me
You'll need to lengthen the sleeves,
My arms are short, the hands already gone,
From felt to baize to nothing—rubbed away,
You'll have to add the lace, and pockets,
Stitch some emblem on the breast,
With a legend—anything
Except death before dishonor will do,
Cut the legs off at the knees,
And put me on, take me off,
Hang me up and say to anyone,
It's not a great coat (and it may be)
But it's a good coat, it will do.
I got it from the poet Flint,
Secondhand but serviceable.
Try it on—it fits almost anyone.
At first look you wouldn't see the reds
So of course it's gray—they were miners
In Wales, West Virginia, Indiana,
Farmers in North Dakota, gray, a little dull.
But he said you'll find the red blood coat
Of the living man, I promise,
If you remember—and wear it well.

Afterward, lying still, sleepy again,
I say tell me to get up and you do
And I sit up, and say, now tell me what to *do*,
And you smile and say, go write a poem.
Well this is my poem of the morning
This morning, when we wake ready
And you say, do you want me on top?
O yes, I say, and we begin.
My poem this morning is especially that
But also it is how you never
Close your eyes but look at me
As we move, even if I close mine, and
It is the way we smile as in a dream
And it is even the way, by now, we
Sometimes speak of this or that
Child or chore in the early going,
And my best poem of the morning,
Even better, I think, again by now,
Than our times and perfect timing,
Is the way of your long hair as it sways,
Touching my face, long and falling down
And smelling not like new-cut clover or hyacinth or
      fern,
But always like a woman's long, clean hair,
Soft across my face and open eyes
And smelling like our life together,
Like morning, this morning, after seven years:
We have written on and in our bodies, love,
The poem of the day, which this can but improve.

AMADEUS QUARTET
(*the day after Yom Kippur, 1978*)

Four old Israelis play violins for Mozart,
Sitting in a semicircle facing me
And they look, altogether,
Like a large Hebrew character upon the stage;
Later I check the dictionary, and yes,
There they are, the Ayin, or Sin, or Shin
(If they were tipped forward a little).
Each man tense, intensely present,
The violin erect before him,
The smaller semicircle of his arms divided
By the violin and moving bow,
So that each man himself
Is a Hebrew character too, maybe the Teth, also
     tipped.

Written in perfect sounds before my eyes:
Five Hebrew characters held by and holding Mozart.

Later one is interviewed and says,
Of course we argue, we argue all the time—
About precisely how to play it—
But to all of us
The intention of the master is sacrosanct.
He is asked if this is not in the Jewish tradition
Of scholarly dispute and commentary on the holy
     books?
Yes, he says, exactly like the Bible:
Beethoven or Mozart—or *God*—said *something*,
What did he say?
Then we sit to play:
And we try to make it be exactly
What (was written down by him)
We call a masterpiece.

I hadn't seen snow in summer
In the forty-three years it's been
Since, early that morning, in North Dakota,
It snowed for an hour on the Fourth of July.
It melted into the season's usual weather,
Into the day's parades, fireworks, and speeches,
So that by evening the snow, like the morning itself,
Was no more than a small boy's dream.
Gone away as that sounds, I can still see snow
Whitely silting the green fields of the farm.
Later, every summer, the tall cottonwoods
Would let fall their snow,
Softer than flakes, more finely formed,
Stuff that moves both up and down
With the lightest breath of moving air,
A snow of dreaming, or the dream itself.
I haven't been back to my hometown
When the cottonwood releases snow
But in June I've come around the world to Varna
And trees here are snowing down
The same fleecy letting go
Of an early harvest in Bulgarian cottonwoods.
The women sweep it up each day,
As we shoveled December walks at home,
But still it makes such drifts
I gathered up three big handfuls
And stuffed the open knot of a tree with it—
I don't know why, some wooly evanescence
Returning snow to the hard tree of ourselves—
As if I were standing here in my own yard
Holding in my open hands this blessing of my journey,
A dry little foam of where I come from,
Where I am today, and where I'm headed in the snow.